BASS BASICS FOR KIDS

:LEARN, PLAY, AND ROCK OUT!!

BASS BASICS FOR KIDS

:LEARN, PLAY, AND ROCK OUT!!

WRITTEN BY KHARI PRATT

Bass Basics for Kids: Learn, Play, and Rock Out!!
Written by Khari Pratt

Copyright © 2025 Khari Pratt
All Rights Reserved.

No part of this book may be copied, stored, or shared in any form without written permission from the author, except for brief excerpts used for educational or review purposes.

ISBN: 979-8-3165-3897-3

This book is dedicated to all young musicians just starting their groove. Keep playing, keep learning, and always have fun with your bass!

Printed in the United States of America.
For more info or permissions, contact:
kharipratt@gmail.com

WHO I AM

Music has been my passion for as long as I can remember. As a bassist, I've helped shape sounds and connect people through rhythm and groove. I'm a founding member of Northeast Groovers and a key part of Mambo Sauce, known for hits like Welcome to D.C. and Miracles. Our music aired on BET, MTV, and VH1, and our debut album, The Recipe, was the highest rated on okayplayer.com in 2009. I've also performed with artists across the country and toured with bands like SOJA.

Now, I'm excited to share what I've learned with the next generation. I created Learn to Groove – A Beginner's Guide to Playing Bass for Kids to teach young musicians the basics of bass and inspire them to find their own sound. Let's make some noise!

DEDICATION

With a big, grateful heart,
I thank God for guiding me every step of the way.
To my wonderful wife, Michelle —
your love and support keep me going. 💖
And to everyone who believed in me —
thank you for cheering me on!
This book wouldn't be possible without you.
Let's keep the music playing! 🎶

TABLE OF CONTENTS

1. Who I Am
2. Dedication
3. Intro Page – Hi There, Future Bass Star!!
4. Let's Meet the Bass Guitar!
5. The 4-String Bass & Fretboard
6. The 5-String Bass & Fretboard
7. The Strings – Each One Makes a Different Note
8. Types of Tuners
9. Tuning Your Bass – Part 1: E, A, D, and G Strings
10. Tuning Your Bass – Part 2: Tuning Made Easy
11. Tuning Your Bass – Part 3: Turning the Pegs for the Right Sound
12. Playing Notes – Press Your Finger on the First Fret
13. Notes on the 4-String Bass
14. Notes on the 5-String Bass
15. How the Bass Sounds – Feel That Groove!
16. The Beat Keeper – Bass Players Keep the Band Moving
17. Playing in a Band – The Bass and Drums Are Best Friends
18. Let's Try a Groove! – Two Notes with Rhythm
19. Keep Practicing! – Every Great Bassist Started Small
20. Pick Up Your Bass, and Let's Keep Rockin'!
21. Draw Your Groove!
22. Keep Strumming and Have Fun
23. The Author

HI THERE, FUTURE BASS STAR!!

LET'S MEET THE BASS GUITAR. IT HAS A LONG NECK, A BODY THAT MAKES SOUND, AND USUALLY JUST FOUR STRINGS E, A, D AND G.

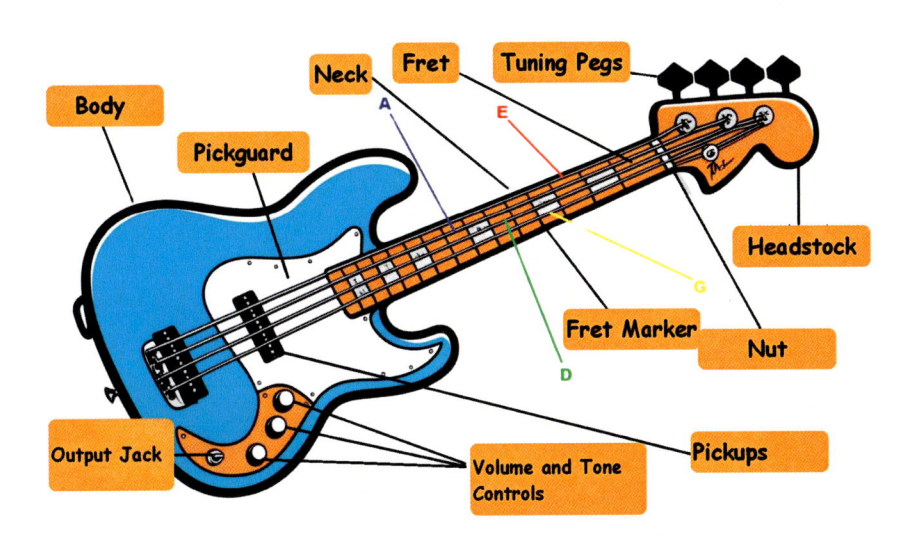

4 STRING BASS AND FRET BOARD

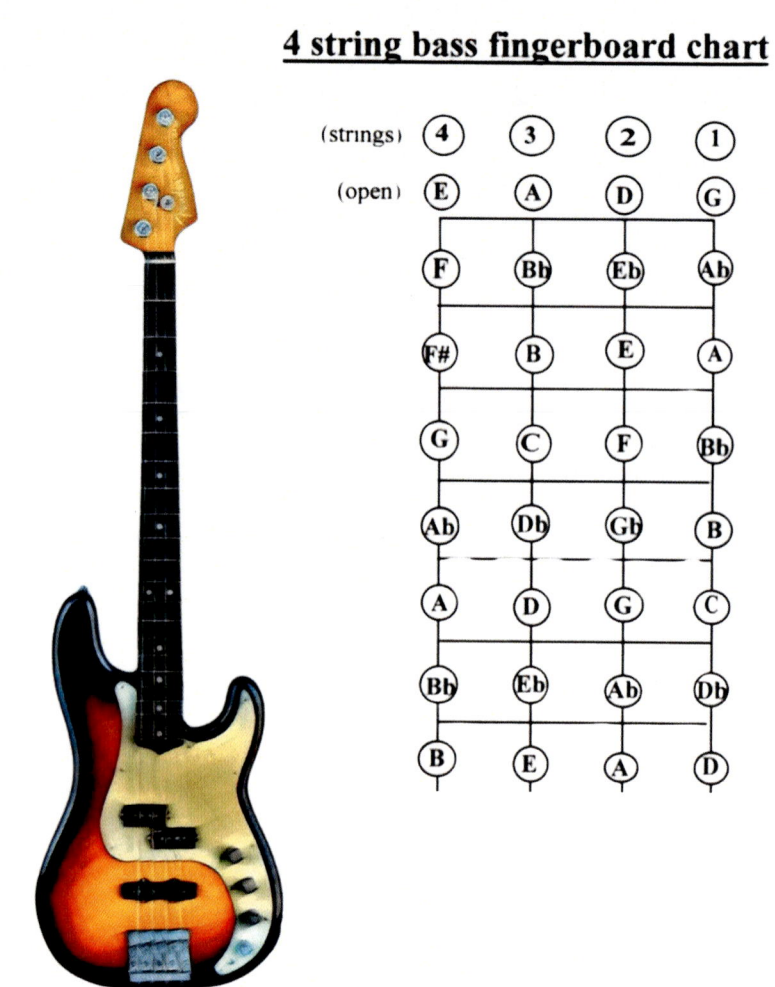

4 string bass fingerboard chart

(strings)	4	3	2	1
(open)	E	A	D	G
	F	Bb	Eb	Ab
	F#	B	E	A
	G	C	F	Bb
	Ab	Db	Gb	B
	A	D	G	C
	Bb	Eb	Ab	Db
	B	E	A	D

5 STRING BASS AND FRETBOARD

5 string bass fingerboard chart

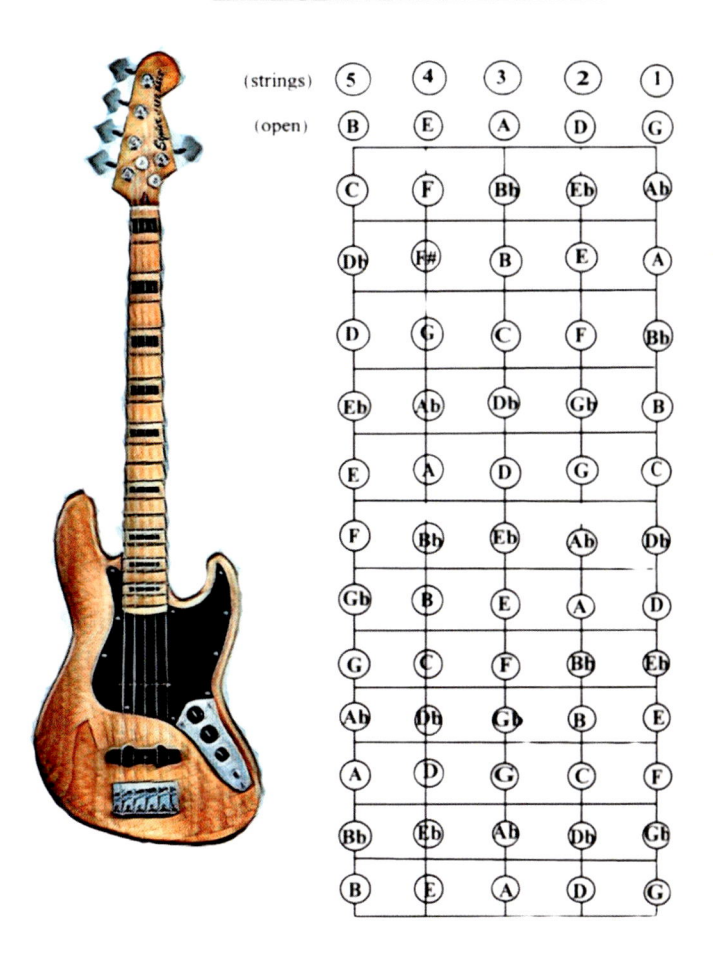

(strings)	5	4	3	2	1
(open)	B	E	A	D	G
	C	F	Bb	Eb	Ab
	Db	F#	B	E	A
	D	G	C	F	Bb
	Eb	Ab	Db	Gb	B
	E	A	D	G	C
	F	Bb	Eb	Ab	Db
	Gb	B	E	A	D
	G	C	F	Bb	Eb
	Ab	Db	Gb	B	E
	A	D	G	C	F
	Bb	Eb	Ab	Db	Gb
	B	E	A	D	G

EACH STRING MAKES A DIFFERENT NOTE — LOW, DEEP SOUNDS THAT YOU FEEL IN YOUR CHEST.
THE STRINGS HAVE NAMES TOO: E, A, D, AND G. SAY IT WITH ME — E, A, D, G!

TYPES OF TUNERS FOR BASS GUITAR

PLUG IN TUNER

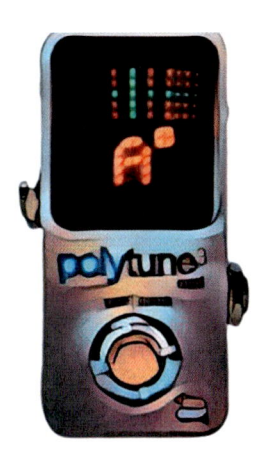

CLIP ON TUNER

PLUG IN PEDAL TUNER

STEP 1

HI THERE, FUTURE ROCK STAR!
YOUR BASS GUITAR HAS FOUR BIG STRINGS,
AND EACH ONE HAS ITS OWN SPECIAL NOTE.
THESE STRINGS ARE NAMED:
- E (THE LOWEST AND THICKEST STRING)
- A
- D
- G (THE HIGHEST AND THINNEST STRING)

A FUN WAY TO REMEMBER THEM IS:
EVERY APPLE DOES GOOD!

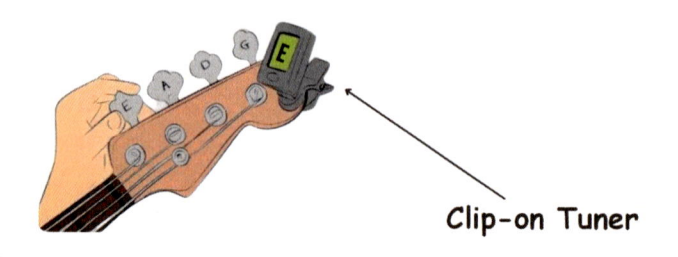

Clip-on Tuner

STEP 2

TUNING YOUR BASS MAKES SURE EACH STRING SOUNDS RIGHT— LIKE SETTING THE TV TO THE PERFECT VOLUME!

YOU'LL NEED A TUNER, LIKE:
- ✅ A CLIP-ON TUNER
- ✅ A PLUG-IN TUNER
- ✅ A BUILT-IN AMP TUNER

LET'S GET YOUR BASS IN TUNE!

STEP 3

LET'S GET STARTED!
PLUCK A STRING AND CHECK THE TUNER.
IF THE NOTE IS TOO LOW (-), TIGHTEN THE PEG.
IF THE NOTE IS TOO HIGH (+), LOOSEN THE PEG.
TUNE EACH STRING ONE AT A TIME IN THIS ORDER: E → A → D → G

LISTEN LIKE A PRO!
YOUR EARS ARE AWESOME TOOLS! TRY LISTENING TO EACH NOTE AND COMPARE IT TO THE CORRECT SOUND.

PRO TIP: IF YOUR BASS SOUNDS WEIRD WHILE PLAYING, CHECK YOUR TUNING AGAIN!
YOU'RE READY TO ROCK!
GREAT JOB! NOW YOUR BASS IS IN TUNE AND READY FOR MUSIC.

THE LOW E STRING IS THE THICKEST STRING ON YOUR BASS GUITAR AND MAKES A DEEP, COOL SOUND LIKE DINOSAUR FOOTSTEPS! YOU DON'T HAVE TO PRESS ANY FRETS TO PLAY IT—JUST PLUCK THE STRING WITH YOUR RIGHT HAND. THE BASS HAS FOUR FUN STRINGS: E, A, D, AND G TRY PLUCKING THEM ALL AND MAKE YOUR BASS GO BOOM... BOOM... BOOM!

IF YOU PRESS YOUR FINGER DOWN ON THE FIRST FRET OF THE E STRING AND PLUCK IT, THAT'S AN F NOTE.
MOVE TO THE THIRD FRET, AND YOU'VE FOUND G. NICE!

"FIVE STRINGS NOW,
LET'S GIVE IT A GO—
PLUCKING FROM TOP TO
LOW!
B E A, D AND G FIVE
FUN NOTES AS HAPPY AS
CAN BE!"

"BASS MAKES DEEP SOUNDS YOU CAN FEEL..."

BASS PLAYERS DON'T JUST PLAY MUSIC — THEY KEEP THE WHOLE BAND MOVING LIKE A TRAIN ON A TRACK.

"NOW LETS PLAY "F" AND "G" NOTES IN A RHYTHM..."

BEFORE   IMPROVES   BETTER

"EVERY GREAT BASSIST STARTED SMALL..."

"NOW LET'S PICK UP YOUR BASS AND KEEP ROCKIN'!"

DRAW YOUR GROOVE!

MAKE YOUR OWN 4-NOTE GROOVE USING ONLY OPEN STRINGS:
DRAW A CIRCLE AROUND THE STRINGS YOU WANT TO PLAY:
E A D G G G!!

[O] E   [ ] A   [ ] D   [O] G
[ ] E   [O] A   [ ] D   [O] G
[ ] E   [ ] A   [O] D   [O] G

"KEEP STRUMMING AND HAVE FUN!"

MUSIC IS AN ADVENTURE, AND EVERY NOTE YOU PLAY IS PART OF YOUR OWN SONG. KEEP PRACTICING, LISTENING, AND ENJOYING YOUR BASS GUITAR. REMEMBER, LOW NOTES BRING DEEP, RICH SOUNDS, WHILE HIGH NOTES ADD BRIGHT, LIVELY TONES—JUST LIKE COLORS IN A PAINTING!

WHAT SONG WILL YOU PLAY NEXT?

THE AUTHOR

INDEX (A-Z)

About the Author – Page 23
Dedication – Page 2
Draw Your Groove! – Page 21
Fretboard (4-String) – Page 5
Fretboard (5-String) – Page 6
How the Bass Sounds – Page 15
Intro – Hi There, Future Bass Star!! – Page 3
Keep Practicing! – Page 19
Keep Strumming and Have Fun – Page 22
Let's Meet the Bass Guitar – Page 4
Let's Try a Groove! – Page 18
Notes on the 4-String Bass – Page 13
Notes on the 5-String Bass – Page 14
Pick Up Your Bass and Let's Keep Rockin'! – Page 20
Playing in a Band – Bass and Drums – Page 17
Playing Notes (First Fret) – Page 12
The Beat Keeper – What Bassists Do – Page 16
The Strings – Each One Makes a Different Note – Page 7
Tuning (Part 1: E, A, D, G Strings) – Page 9
Tuning (Part 2: Made Easy) – Page 10
Tuning (Part 3: Turning the Pegs) – Page 11
Tuners – Types of – Page 8
Who I Am – Page 1

Thank You for Grooving With Me!
Thank you so much for picking up Bass Basics for Kids: Learn, Play, and Rock Out!
It means the world to me to share my love of music—and especially the bass guitar—with you. I've spent my life playing, performing, and making funky, feel-good music with amazing bands, and now I'm so excited to help you start your musical journey.
Whether you're just learning your first notes or already jamming with friends, I hope this book helps you feel confident, creative, and ready to groove.
So thank you—for reading, for learning, and for making music a part of your life. I can't wait to hear about all the amazing things you'll do!
Stay groovy, keep practicing, and most of all... have fun!

Made in United States
Orlando, FL
18 July 2025